My Country
Egypt

Jillian Powell

W
FRANKLIN WATTS
LONDON•SYDNEY

First published in 2012
by Franklin Watts

Copyright © Franklin Watts 2012

Franklin Watts
338 Euston Road
London NW1 3BH

Franklin Watts Australia
Level 17/207 Kent Street
Sydney, NSW 2000

All rights reserved

Dewey number: 962'.056
ISBN: 978 1 4451 1049 3

Printed in China

Series Editor: Paul Rockett
Series Designer: Paul Cherrill
  for Basement68
Picture Researcher: Diana Morris

Franklin Watts is a division of
Hachette Children's Books,
an Hachette UK company.

www.hachette.co.uk

Every attempt has been made to clear copyright.
Should there be any inadvertent omission please apply
to the publisher for rectification.

Picture credits: Albo/Shutterstock: 11; Atlaspix/Shutterstock: 4b,
22c; Baloncici/Dreamstime: 5; Dan Breckwoldt/Shutterstock: 2,
20; Tiziano Casalta/Dreamstime: 8; Carlos Cazals/Corbis: 14;
Jean Dominique Dallet/Alamy: 15c; dbimages/Alamy: front cover c,
4t, 13b inset, 15b, 19b, 22t; David Forman/Latitudestock/Alamy:
9t; Jeremy Graham/Alamy: 21; Janthon Jackson/Dreamstime:
6; John James/Alamy: 12; Frans Lemmens/Alamy: 19c; Christine
Osborne/World Religions PL/Alamy: 18; Ilene Perlman/Alamy: 17;
PictureContact BV/Alamy: 13; sculpies/Shutterstock: front cover
r; slava296/Shutterstock: 9b; Verdelho/Dreamstime: 7; Nickolay
Vinokurov/Shutterstock: 3, 10; Stuart Westmorland/Corbis: front
cover l; Zurijeta/Shutterstock: 1, 16.

 Contents

All words in **bold**
appear in the
glossary on page 23.

Egypt in the world

My name is Hassan and I come from Egypt.

Egypt is in two **continents**. Most of the country is in North Africa but the eastern part is in Asia.

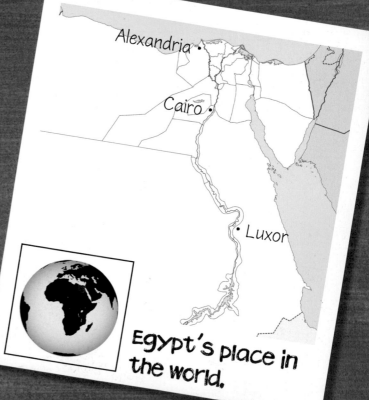

Alexandria

Cairo

Luxor

Egypt's place in the world.

4

I live in Cairo, which is the capital city of Egypt. It is the biggest city in Africa and is always busy with people and traffic.

Rush hour traffic in Cairo.

5

People who live in Egypt

People in Egypt speak and write **Arabic**, though we often understand and speak English or French too. Many are Muslims but there are also Christians.

Fishermen on the Nile, using nets to catch fish.

Most people live close to the river Nile where they can find work in the cities or in farming and fishing.

There are jobs in **tourism** and in factories that make oil, chemicals, cloth and food products.

Tourists visiting the Great Pyramid of Giza.

Egypt's landscape

Most of Egypt's land is **desert**.

The river Nile separates the Eastern and Western Deserts.

Sand dunes in the Sahara Desert. The Western Desert is part of the Sahara.

Farmland is mainly along the river Nile and the river **delta**. Farmers grow crops of cotton, sugar cane, rice and oranges.

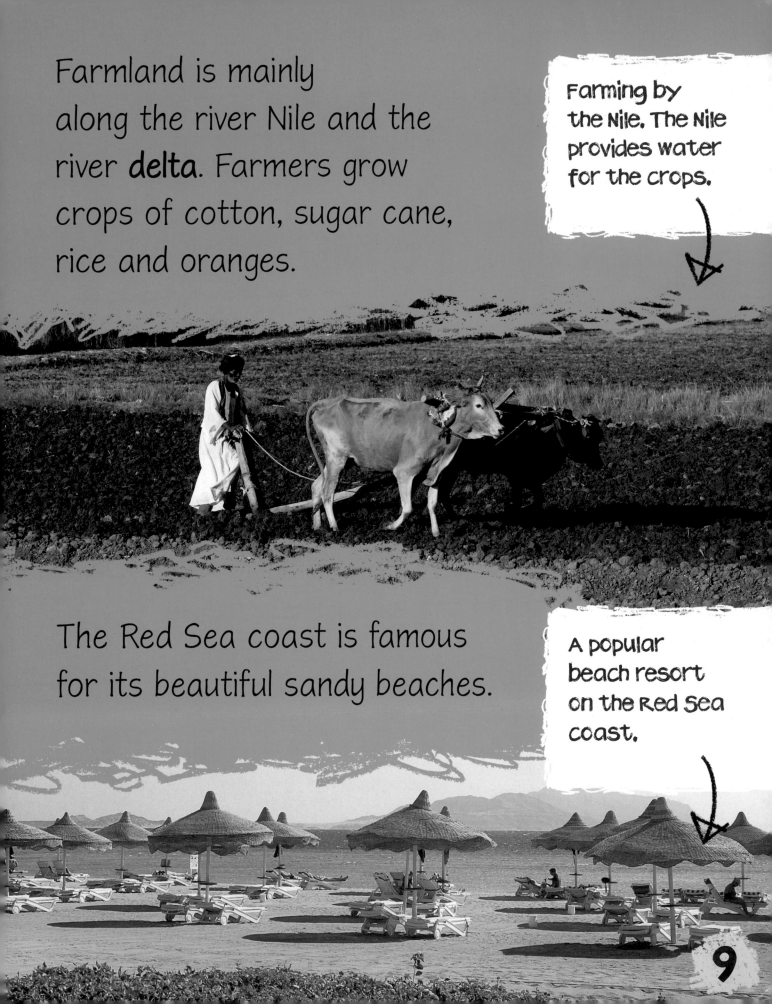

The Red Sea coast is famous for its beautiful sandy beaches.

9

 # The weather in Egypt

People riding camels through a desert storm.

The weather in Egypt is mostly hot and dry all year round. In April, hot dusty winds blow in from the Sahara Desert.

The hottest months are in summer between June and August. Winters, from November to February, are usually mild and cloudy.

Sunset over the Nile.

At home with my family

I live with my family in an apartment in Cairo. We have a big living room at the front, a kitchen, bathroom and three bedrooms. My grandparents live a few blocks away.

We live on the ninth floor, so we have a good view over the city.

At home I enjoy watching television or playing computer games. Sometimes we go to the cinema to see a film.

Family is very important. Our cousins visit us a lot.

I like playing soccer with my friends.

What we eat

In the evening, families sit down for a meal together.

At breakfast, we usually eat bread and honey, or boiled eggs and some fruit.

The main meal is usually a spicy dish of meat or vegetables, with rice and bread.

In the evening, we have **mezze**, which are different dishes and dips that we eat with flat bread, using the bread and our right hand to scoop up food.

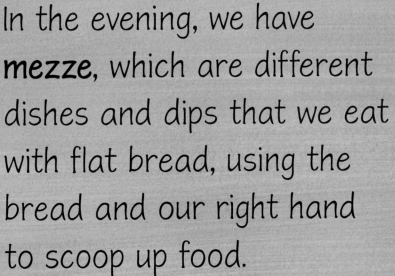

Mezze can be made up of hot or cold dishes.

My favourite food is ice cream!

15

Going to school

Most children in Egypt go to school from the age of six years old. At primary school, we have lessons in maths, reading and writing.

we read Arabic writing from the right to the left on a page.

16

In the third year, we begin science lessons.

we read The Qu'ran daily.

Muslim children, like me, also have lessons in the holy book of Islam, **The Qu'ran**.

festivals and celebrations

We celebrate the first day of spring in March with picnics and boat trips on the Nile.

Street stalls along the Nile during the Spring Festival.

Eid-al-Fitr is an important Muslim festival. Families get together to feast and have fun after the month of **Ramadan**.

camel racing is a popular sport during Eid.

At Eid, we usually go to the funfair.

Things to see

Many people come to see the pyramids at Giza. They were built for the **pharaohs** or kings over 4,000 years ago.

The pyramids are one of the Seven wonders of the world.

People also like to take a cruise boat down the river Nile, and visit the **bazaars** where they can buy rugs, bags and jewellery.

The Great Bazaar in Cairo.

21

Here are some facts about my country!

Fast facts about Egypt

Capital city = Cairo
Population = 84.5 million
Area = 386,874km^2
Main language = Arabic
National holiday = Revolution Day
Currency = Egyptian pound
Major religions = Islam, Christianity
Longest river = the Nile (6,670km)
Highest mountain = Mount Catherine (2,642m)

Glossary

Arabic the language of the Arab peoples

bazaars markets selling lots of different kinds of goods

continents main land masses of the world

delta flat land at the mouth of a river

desert dry area of land that gets little or no rain

mezze several small dishes of hot and cold foods

pharaohs kings of ancient Egypt

Ramadan ninth month in the Muslim calendar, when people fast (go without food) during the day

The Qu'ran the sacred book of Islam

tourism industry serving visitors and holidaymakers

Websites

http://news.bbc.co.uk/cbbcnews/hi/newsid_4090000/
newsid_4096800/4096826.stm

Cbbc's newsround country profile of Egypt.

www.kidcyber.com.au/topics/egypt.htm

Facts about living in modern Egypt.

www.touregypt.net/featurestories/children.htm

Information about daily lives of children living in Egypt.

Books

Countries of the World: Egypt (National Geographic Society, 2007)

River Adventures: Nile by Paul Manning (Franklin Watts, 2012)

Everyday History: Life in Ancient Egypt by Nathaniel Harris (Franklin Watts, 2007)

Index